1/79

THE PEOPLE & PLACES OF JAMAICA

THE PEOPLE & PLACES OF JAMAICA

Principal photography
NICOLAI CANETTI

Commentary
SANDY LESBERG

A HADDINGTON HOUSE BOOK

Distributed by THE BOBBS-MERRILL CO., INC.

FIRST PUBLISHED 1976 BY
PEEBLES PRESS INTERNATIONAL
12 Thayer St., London W1M 5LD
10 Columbus Circle, New York, N.Y. 10019

Designed by Nicolai Canetti

© Peebles Press International (Europe) Ltd
ISBN 0–672–52259–4
Library of Congress Catalog No. 76–10525

The publishers wish to acknowledge with great gratitude
the splendid assistance and co-operation they have received
in the preparation of this book from the Jamaica Tourist Board.

Distributed by
The Bobbs-Merrill Co. Inc.
4300 West 62nd St., Indianapolis, Indiana 46268, U.S.A.
in the United States and Canada

Printed and bound in the U.K. by
Redwood Burn Limited, Trowbridge and Esher

There is such a thing in life called presence. Unseen but felt, undefined but real. Here, in Jamaica, no matter how bright the day, how lush the green foliage and trees, how quiet the blue-green Caribbean water, how majestic the hills, there are certain times of your stay when you are suddenly and inexplicably engulfed by wondrous feelings that are not to be found in any other place you may visit.

Perhaps it is the seemingly inexhaustible torrent of visual beauty on the island, and the presence is gay and uplifting. Perhaps you are touched by the fringes of *obeah*, Jamaican voodoo, a practice forbidden by law but acknowledged to exist as a perpetual, albeit sub rosa, influence that permeates the life of the people in the hills while certainly touching the city folk as well. Perhaps one day here you are subdued, quiet, uncharacteristically pensive. Perhaps you are skimming the edges of *obeah*.

Jamaica then is unique because there is the look of it and there is very much the feel of it, too.

Two hundred years ago the slaves revolted and went into the hills, some gathering in the east near Port Antonio, some in the Cockpit Country farther to the west. The soldiers who were despatched to recapture these newly born free souls soon learned that on the days when the sky was cloudless and the forests most peaceful it was then that they should heed the advice of their superiors to "look behind" them at all times in order to protect themselves against the strange and wondrous assaults that invariably took place. Those parts of Jamaica are still called the "land of look behind" and it seems an apt description of the country. It is genuinely a place to toss off the vestments, both psychological and physical, of the outside world and submerge into what must be a totally unique experience. It is a sensory delight to experience the visions of the eye while at the same time sinking into the beautiful nonspecific feelings of mystery and excitement that permeate the very air of the place.

And, of course, there are the people. Look at the faces of Jamaica and you will find reflected there the great hidden treasures of a multitude of ancient races and civilisations. China, Africa, Scotland, India – from all over the world arrived the travellers, slaves, commercial men, sailors – all coming together to form the unique beauty of the Jamaican people of today.

So there is the look of the place, and the feel of it, and the fantastic people, and also the remarkable frivolous tropical wind with a style of its own that arrives quite without warning, clutching handfuls of trees in its path, selecting with a true course only the ones it wishes to impress and ignoring all the others. Sometimes it carries the rain with it and if it is in a proper mood it will sweep up one side of the road and leave the other side virtually untouched, as if to disdain the broad strokes for the more subtle and more telling one. Once observed, this high tropical wind of Jamaica, you will not be quick to forget it.

Jamaica is a thoroughly unique experience – lovely, volatile, mysterious, capable of creating in you feelings of deep happiness and joy tinged with vague stirrings of disquiet. Different. Attractive. Seductive. Unforgettable.

Jamaica.

Age is no factor in owning a shop in Montego Bay

PRECEDING PAGE: The Salvation Army
band at the Ocho Rios open market

Street faces, Montego Bay . . .

14

Women of Jamaica

Dunn's River Falls (also on previous page)

Dunn's River Falls

A village in the mountains

PRECEDING PAGE: A rafting tour on the Martha Brae River

Harvesting coconuts

A "higgler" woman (vendor) on Saturday market day

The older generation

Glass bottom boat – near Montego Bay

Friendship Pimento Estate, Reading

A North Coast beach

Typical coral reef

Child with pimento flowers — used for allspice

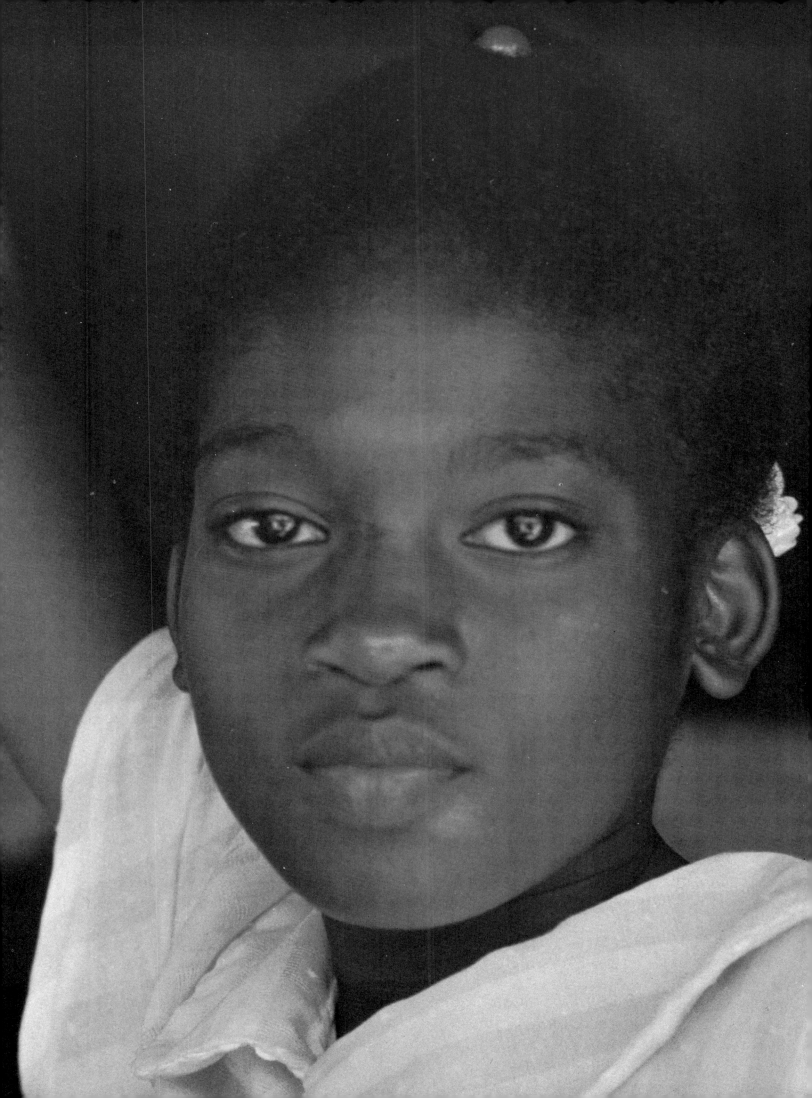

A racing steed at the Friendship Pimento Estate

OVERLEAF: Do their names match their faces —
on the left, Mischief, on the right, Jasmine

Girls go to school in the mountains

... And they pass the Court House, Port Antonio, on their way to school, too

Eating sugar cane in the mountains

OPPOSITE PAGE:
The blue waters by the caves of Negril

Playing marbles . . .
. . . And cards

Street scenes, Montego Bay

PRECEDING PAGE, LEFT: Revival cult ritual called *pocomania.* Leading the ritual is
the shepherd of the cult, Kapo, who is a primitive painter.
PRECEDING PAGE, RIGHT: A fire-eater

Market scene of Jamaican home grown fruits and vegetables.
Typical ones include: cho cho, callalu, paw paw (Jamaican for
papaya), bread fruit and root vegetables.

The law surveys his beat

Woodcarver at the Ocho Rios market

Maroons preparing for a traditional dance in camouflaged costumes
which portray the guerrilla warfare they once used against
the planters

OPPOSITE PAGE: Relaxing in Negril

Newspaper boy in Montego Bay

Brewing the tea in Montego Bay market

Wherever a large haul of fish is netted an impromptu fish market is set up on shore. Fishermen clean and sell the fish right on the spot.

Fish market scenes . . .

Bananas carried in the traditional manner